Praying Through the Seven Mountains

By Jeremy & Janna Butrous
Illustrations By E.M.M Clonts

© Copyright 2014 by Jeremy Butrous.

All rights reserved. This book is protected by the copyright laws of the United States of America. This book may not be copied or reprinted for commercial gain or profit. The use of short quotations or occasional page copying for personal or group study is permitted and encouraged.

Scripture quotations are taken from the New American Standard Bible®, Copyright © 1960, 1962, 1963, 1968, 1971, 1972, 1973, 1975, 1977, 1995 by The Lockman Foundation. Used by permission. http://www.lockman.org/

Scripture quoted by permission. Quotations designated (NET) are from the NET Bible®. Copyright ©1996-2006 by Biblical Studies Press, LLC http://netbible.com. All rights reserved.

ISBN 978-0-9912355-0-6

Printed in the United States.

Table of Contents

1. Endorsements..5
2. Context for the Parents..7
3. Suggested Use of This Book...9
4. 7 Mountain School..11
5. Mountain of Education..14
6. Mountain of Government..26
7. Mountain of Religion..38
8. Mountain of Media...50
9. Mountain of Economy..62
10. Mountain of Family..74
11. Mountain of Celebration...86
12. Back to Class..98
13. Glossary...100

Thank you Johnny Enlow and Lance Wallnau for your leadership in communicating the Seven Mountain message.

Thank you Pastor Bill Johnson for showing me what our Father is like, and for gifting me with so much of your time.

Thank you Bob Hartley for showing me that God is not stuck inside a church, but loves to be in all of life.

Thank you Sandra Backman for your wonderful perspective in this project.

Thank you Holy Spirit for teaching me about Jesus and showing me how a hardworking carpenter changed the world through obedience to His Father.

Endorsements

In Matthew 5-7, we find Jesus' very first recorded message, known to most as The Beatitudes. In reality, the very Son of God was providing us with the mission statement of the Trinity. Almost immediately Jesus began to speak of inheriting the earth and blessing those with a heart for mercy, justice, and righteousness on earth, as well as the "peacemakers." He then went on to say, "You are the salt of the earth... and the light of the world," confirming that our mission is not simply to get converts for eternity, but rather partners in spreading His rule and reign on earth. In Matthew 5:15, Jesus further elaborated on the mission of being light by saying it must be on a lamp stand or candlestick- it must provide enough light for a city. For the Jewish population the picture that would come immediately to mind would be the 7 branched candlestick, a menorah. In essence, the instructive assignment given to us by Jesus Himself was to provide 7 identifiable forms of light that would bring wisdom that an entire society could operate from. I believe these 7 branches to represent the 7 mountains mentioned in Revelation 17:9 that are ultimately connected to revealing the 7 forms of light that come from the 7 spirits of God mentioned in Revelation 4:5 and 5:6. These 7 primary areas of culture in every society are: government, media, education, family, economy, celebration (arts and entertainment), and religion (worship). The sons and daughters of God are receiving much present illumination on this assignment and it is creating a vital, wholesale paradigm shift so that we may return to the original commission established not just by the law or prophets or other great men of God, but by Jesus Himself.

Furthermore, before Jesus finished with that first message, He gave us the often memorized and greatly quoted "Lord's Prayer" of Matthew 6: 6-15. The instruction here was that "when you pray" to pray the full implications of verse 10, "Your kingdom come Your will be done, on earth as it is in heaven." Jesus did not come to earth with only exit strategies- or how to wait to be rescued. This passage was the exclamation point to the Magna Carta Jesus began His ministry with, which was to see heaven brought to earth. We have, for various reasons, lost that initial message, and instead prioritized how to make it OUT of this earth. I believe we are in a season as a generation where we are now understanding that we must agree with Jesus' passion to see heaven come down TO earth and for us to be His partners in receiving the kingdom of God, accessing His better ways of doing everything.

With this new understanding as a back drop, we see the profound importance of teaching our children early instruction in agreeing and cooperating with this original mission. The paradigm shifting must begin from as early an age as possible and there is no better way for that to happen than to walk with our children through praying into these 7 primary areas of society. Jeremy served me as a personal assistant for a year and a half as we traveled all over the globe preaching and teaching on the 7 mountains. He had a front row view and back stage pass, so to speak, at how this message energized the church into the excitement of our original assignment. It gives me great pleasure to see what Jeremy and Janna have written and I am happy to endorse this remarkable endeavor to begin connecting our children with their Savior's passion for bringing "heaven on earth." I truly believe that as our kids begin to pray into these mountains of inheritance, it will begin to open their minds and spirits to not only pray with conviction, but to also have a healthy desire to actually receive the kingdom in whatever area of society they ultimately are called to serve in. Therefore, it is my privilege to praise this one-of-a-kind effort and to desire that every kingdom-minded parent would use this as a tool to assist their child in connecting to our mission and their unique destiny in it.

Johnny Enlow
Speaker and Author
The Seven Mountain Prophecy, The Seven Mountain Mandate

Jeremy and Janna Butrous have written a wonderful children's book about adventure; but this adventure is not for the faint of heart. Such a journey could actually have an effect on the course of history. In Praying through the 7 Mountains, children are taught how to pray and influence the various realms of culture and society. I love when the rich assignments of God are broken down into bite-sized pieces that children can receive, because they don't have a junior Holy Spirit. The authors have succeeded in taking big ideas and making them doable for very young world-changers. Parents, get ready to be challenged, and get ready to help lead a generation who actually believe that nothing is impossible with God.

Bill Johnson
Bethel Church, Redding, CA
Author—Hosting the Presence

Praying through the 7 Mountains by Jeremy Butrous is a fantastic book! It is beautifully written and illustrated and will open children's eyes to the world around them. It teaches children to honor and value workers in each sector of society as they read about the giftings and talents required for each field. God calls us to pray for our leaders and for one another; this book makes it easy and accessible for parents or teachers to pray specific, powerful prayers for people in each of the 7 mountains with the children in their lives. I pray that intercession will rise from children around the world and bless Papa God's heart. I love Jeremy's vision to teach our children to dream big and influence every area of society with God's love and for His glory. Everywhere I go, I always ask the children I meet what their dreams are. In Mozambique, children are most excited to be teachers, nurses, construction workers, soccer players, and presidents--it was fabulous to find each of those jobs in this book! Once children receive the Father heart and move from an orphan spirit to a spirit of sonship, they too want to influence a nation. I pray that God will use this book to encourage children to follow God's calling and have a broader perspective of the world. I bring the Children's Adoration Prayer Book to the villages with me each week and pray with our children. I look forward to bringing this book with me as well to pray about their dreams and to pray for people in each mountain of society to be true world changers for Jesus.

Heidi G. Baker, PhD
Co-Founder and Director of Iris Global

Context for the Parents

Life on Earth is a gift from our Father in Heaven. It is a beautiful treasure that we get to explore and enjoy. Every person has been created by God and birthed into humanity for a reason. What is the purpose for us to have this earthly experience? Many Christians would say that our life's purpose is to realize our need for a savior, receive salvation, and wait for Jesus to return.

Eternal security through salvation is a promise from Jesus. This security is absolute, certain for those who are sealed unto the day of Redemption. There is no question about the return of the Lord. It is God's job to return; it is our job to find out why we are alive.

The question for each of us to ask is, "What will I do until He returns?" The big picture to this question is answered in the command of the Lord spoken to us before He left the Earth.

What will we do until He returns?
Christ desires for us to disciple nations.
"Go therefore and make disciples of all the nations" (Matthew 28:19).

Why would we want to disciple nations?
The Earth is our inheritance, yet there is a purpose in this: God wants us to partner with Him.
"Blessed are the gentle, for they shall inherit the earth" (Matthew 5:5).

How do we make disciples of all nations?
We actively apply the Lord's Prayer, Matthew 6:10, through everyday life.
"Your kingdom come. Your will be done, on Earth as it is in heaven."

We must understand the identity of a nation to disciple it. Each nation can be defined by seven categories of society that are outlined in the Bible. The seven areas encompass every person and occupation. They are listed below in no particular order and defined in this book as the "Seven Mountains."
1. Education
2. Government
3. Religion
4. Media
5. Economy
6. Family
7. Celebration

God wants us to bring change and discipleship to the world. By applying our gifts, callings, and areas of influences, we can become the change that the world needs at any age!

Biblical Context for the Seven Mountains

Each Mountain is topically referred to throughout the Bible. The only place you will find the Seven Mountains congruently is in the book of Revelation, in a passage referring to "the harlot and the beast."
"The seven heads are seven Mountains on which the woman is seated" (Revelation 17:9)
"And the woman that you saw is the great city that has dominion over the kings of the earth" (Revelation 17:18).

These passages can be seen as an invitation for us bring influence and change to the Seven Mountains. If we neglect to do so, evil will become the predominant influence in this world.

Biblical Context for Discipling Nations

Do you recall the passage in the Bible when Satan came and tempted Jesus?
"Again, the devil took Him up to an exceedingly high Mountain, and showed Him all the kingdoms of the world and their glory. And he said to Him, "All these things I will give You, if You will fall down and worship me." Then Jesus said to him, "Away with you. Satan! For it is written, 'You shall worship the Lord your God, and him only you shall serve." Then the devil left Him, and behold, angels came and ministered to him" (Matthew 4:8).

Why would the devil offer Jesus the kingdoms of the world and their glory? The devil was never given anything except what he gained from Adam and Eve in the garden. He stole the kingdoms of the world and their glory from humanity. The devil did not steal souls; he stole the kingdoms of the world that rightfully belonged to the children of God. The kingdoms of the world were rightfully given to us from our Father so that we can rule and reign with Him.

When Jesus rose from the dead, He returned to us all authority and restored the relationship that humanity had with God in the Garden of Eden. Our role in life is not to just go to Heaven, but to rule and reign with God on earth. We must see this as essential purpose for living. We are to give Jesus the greatest gift humanity could ever give God – a redeemed earth.

Passion for Praying through the Seven Mountains
(A Note from Jeremy Butrous)

Children try to act like heroes such as Superman, the president, or an army soldier. Why? As parents and teachers, we tell our children to reach for the moon. We tell them to dream of a bright future and have hope. Those dreams are never supposed to go away. Our children may not become Superman when they grow up, but they can become the greatest possible version of themselves (which is even better)!

God has given each one of us a specific set of gifts, callings and abilities. He has placed the Seven Mountains in the heart of man. There is a perfect model for Education, Government, Religion, Media, Economy, Family, and Celebration in Heaven that He wants to show us. He has hopeful eyes for humanity and wants us to use them. God speaks to His children ideas from His heart and plans of success. He gives us solutions to the world's problems for every aspect of life.

You can help your child become one of the greatest investment bankers, dancers, hair stylists, or movie producers. They could become the best mother or father, politician, or receptionist – from the bottom of the Mountain all the way to the top. It is our goal to teach our children to bring change in every area of life. This book is designed to proclaim the truth that everyone can be great. We can teach our children to help many people and save many lives. We can raise our children to disciple nations. We can raise our children to be free to dream! Our children will be "Children with Purpose!"

Suggested Use of This Book

This book was written to help your children begin their own personal journey to encounter the God of all life. **Praying through the Seven Mountains** can be used alongside any regular Bible reading or family devotional time. This book is designed to enable your child or student to discover God and him or herself in everyday life on the Seven Mountains, and to have a hopeful perspective for the people around them. My prayer is that they will grow in their God-given destiny.

The Seven Mountains will be introduced in a school session with Miss Fitzgerald. Your child or student will learn about the Seven Mountains of Life along with seven students, each from a different continent. Miss Fitzgerald will introduce the Seven Mountains to the class through a new curriculum that they will be learning. The school context will start at the beginning of the book and will conclude at the end. The class session provides a fun and gentle way to introduce the curriculum of the book to your child or student.
Praying through the Seven Mountains will have four main components to each page:
Personal Representative
Supporting Scripture
Heaven's Thoughts
Let's Pray Together.

Personal Representative - Each Mountain will have five Personal Representatives. They are not exhaustive in any way, but they serve as a glimpse of what type of person or occupation might represent that Mountain. This book will contain 35 Personal Representatives.

Supporting Scripture - Each Supporting Scripture is a biblical reference to help show you and your child or student the heart of God as it pertains to the Mountain and Personal Representative. Each scripture becomes the invitation to live by. The book contains one scripture per page. Feel free to discover more scriptures on your own for each Mountain.

Heaven's Thoughts - Heaven's Thoughts is designed for your child or student to see the best traits and characteristics in the Personal Representatives. It outlines the most hopeful perspective, describing Heaven's views towards that Mountain or Personal Representative. The intent of Heaven's Thoughts is to introduce hopeful perspectives and reinforce the knowledge of God. It is our hope and prayer that you and your child or student would be filled with hopeful eyes towards every person on every Mountain.

Let's Pray Together - This section gives you a wonderful opportunity to pray through scripture and Heaven's Thoughts. Let's Pray Together is a thankful prayer time that opens up the heart of your child or student. During this time, your child or student will be welcoming Heaven's attributes and God's heart of the Personal Representative. They will also pray for those attributes and characteristics to be shown in their own life. Lastly, they will pray for the Personal Representative that is currently active in their life. Be encouraged to add your own prayers to bring practical application in this section.

*Please note that the examples displayed from Scripture, Heaven's Thoughts and Let's Pray Together may differ from your child or student's current life situations or circumstances. The goal of this book is to give the most hopeful picture to the reader. Please encourage them to see what is possible in their own Personal Representatives.

Seven Mountain School

Welcome to Miss Fitzgerald's fifth grade class. The students have just begun a new school year. Their school is located in Los Angeles County in California. Miss Fitzgerald has been teaching for 15 years. She loves teaching and she loves each new class of students that she teaches. This year, new students from different continents are about to discover something they have never known before. Let's join them and find out what it is!

A lady walked to the front of the classroom. She was not much taller than her students. Her brown hair was pulled into a high ponytail and she had a kind smile on her face. "Hello everyone." The students, who had been chatting excitedly, quieted down. "My name is Miss Fitzgerald."

"Hello, Miss Fitzgerald," the students chorused together. "I am very excited about this school year with you," Miss Fitzgerald continued. "Why don't we begin by introducing ourselves so we can get to know each other? Is that okay class?

"Yes, Miss Fitzgerald," the students said. One by one, the fifth graders stood and said their name and a little bit about themselves.

"It looks like some of you are from different continents. That is very interesting. It is wonderful to have so many of you coming from different places. Omari, from the continent of Africa, said he just came to America with his family. Bjorg, from the continent of Antartica, is living with his grandma this year, here in California. Qiang, from the continent of Asia, said she has been living here since she was six years old. Lachlan, from the Australian continent, moved here with his mother last year. This is just wonderful, to have such a variety of students this year.

There were two more students who introduced themselves as having come from another country. Who were they again?" Miss Fitzgerald asked.

One student stood up. His hair was dark and he smiled shyly. "I am from South America," he said. "My name is Santiago."

"Welcome, Santiago."

"And I was born in Europe," said a girl who also stood. "My name is Emma."

"Nice to have you with us, Emma. And the rest of us are from North America. We live in North America. This is going to be a very exciting year. I would like to teach you a new phrase to tell each other, as a way to welcome everyone into this class. It goes like this: This is our class. We are glad to be here. We can all be friends. It is going to be a great year. Do you think you can all say that?"

The students chorused the welcome phrase together, along with Miss Fitzgerald.

"This year we are going to be learning about the Seven Mountains of life. As I pass out your new textbooks, I will tell you a little bit about these Seven Mountains."

Lachlan, the student from Australia, spoke up. "Aren't there more than seven mountains in the world?" "Yes, you're right," Miss Fitzgerald answered. "There are more than seven mountains, but the mountains I am talking about are a little different. You can see by the title of the book, Praying through the Seven Mountains, that these mountains are special. I believe that this book will help you grow in so many new ways, and to look at life from a new and fresh perspective. I want you all to begin looking at the world through the eyes of Heaven. This book is meant to help you discover the treasure that God has placed in the people around you and to help you unlock the wonderful gifts and callings in your own life."

The students looked at each other excitedly. This definitely was not going to be a normal year.

"I want you to find out what Heaven says about the Seven Mountains, and for you to find out what Mountain you like the best. I want you to be inspired and dream of becoming anyone you want to be. Praying through the Seven Mountains will show you seven groups of people that can change the world. I want you to know who they are so that you can also become a world changer. World changers are people that love one another. They are people that care for God's heart to be known. They are people that care for the earth and want everyone to live a happy and healthy life. Praying through the Seven Mountains can help you see a hopeful perspective about everyone. It is important to be hopeful about every person that you meet because every person has been put on Earth for a special reason and God loves every one of us. Now who here wants to be a world changer?" Everyone shouted together, "I do!"

"What do you want to be?" Miss Fitzgerald asked with a smile.

"A World Changer!" The students answered enthusiastically.

"That's wonderful! Now, let's begin to learn about the Seven Mountains. At the beginning of the book you will find instructions for your parents on how to Pray through the Seven Mountains. You can show them the book when you get home. Today, I will tell you why the Seven Mountains are important. Zoey, would you like to come up and write the Seven Mountains on the chalkboard?"

"Sure," Zoey answered. She walked to the front of the class and picked up a stick of white chalk.

"Zoey, you can write down the name of each Mountain as I explain a little bit about them. In this book, the Mountains represent groups of people. The first group of people, which we will call the first Mountain, is the Mountain of Education. This is the Mountain that you are experiencing right now. Education is any time that you are learning, especially at school. In your book you will read about five people in Education. These five people are just a sample of everyone that works in the field of Education. The most important thing about Education is it teaches people skills that help them have a better life."

Miss Fitzgerald then asked her students, "Do you like to learn? Do you want to help teach the world to be a better place?"

"Yes, Miss Fitzgerald," the fifth graders responded enthusiastically.

"That's wonderful. So do I. We will learn more about education in the book. Maybe one of you would like to grow up and be the best professor, principal, or coach there ever was."

"I want to be a professor, like my grandfather," said Santiago."

"That would be amazing!" Miss Fitzgerald said. "God wants to help you do that. The second Mountain is the Mountain of Government. This Mountain is the place where all of our laws come from. Leaders across our city, state and country are in the Mountain of Government. The Mountain of Government is very important. It provides safety and protection from people who try to harm others. The Government also helps give us a peaceful city because of its workers and helpful laws. Don't you want to learn more about government and see how God is using people to bring about good change in the world? Would you like to help make our cities and states a safer place?"

Many of the students nodded. "My father works in the government," Zoey said.

"Good, and maybe one of you will feel called to the Mountain of Government when you grow up.

"The third Mountain is the Mountain of Religion. Religion allows people to learn about God. The people that work at your church are under the Mountain of Religion. They care about God's heart and His people all the time. Do you talk about Jesus all of the time? Maybe you would like to grow up and work in the Mountain of Religion. Learning about God helps you have a better life. Everyone is blessed by the Mountain of Religion."

"I want to teach others about God," said Qiang. "A lot of people in the country I come from don't know very much about God. Maybe I can go back and share it with them."

"That would be wonderful, Qiang," said her teacher.

"Our fourth Mountain is the Mountain of Media. Media is communication through technology. Media helps provide you with your favorite TV shows and movies. We will get to learn about five of the many groups of people that work in the Mountain of Media. Do you ever think about making a movie with some of your friends? Do you have a favorite Cartoon or TV show?"

"I like The Story Keepers," said Emma. "It would be fun to make cartoons about Jesus' life."
"Well, maybe you will be the next great director and everyone will like your movies."
Emma laughed, and Miss Fitzgerald continued. "The fifth Mountain is the Mountain of Economy. The Mountain of Economy is where people build businesses and make money. Every country has an economy, and every country needs help growing their economy. Do you like to go out and shop with your family and friends? Do you like to go shopping? Then you know about the Mountain of Economy. Have you ever thought about having your own shop, where you can sell the things that you make?"
"My big sister found a job in a bookstore. I went there last week to buy a Bible," Lachlan told the teacher.
"That is nice. Maybe one day you can be a business owner that helps the economy grow."
"The sixth Mountain is the Mountain of Family. Everything that relates to family is under this Mountain. Your mother and father are in the Mountain of Family. Family is a wonderful place to grow and celebrate life with people that God gave you. Families are not perfect but everyone can help make them look more like heaven. Do you dream about being a mother or father to your own children one day?"
"I have a big family," Omari spoke up. "I have four sisters and three brothers. I would like to have a big family also."
"Well, then it would be good for you to learn more about the Mountain of Family, I think." Miss Fitzgerald smiled and the students laughed. Omari laughed along with them.
"The seventh and last Mountain is the Mountain of Celebration. Celebration is where people come to have fun with life. Celebration is known for all of the dancers and singers and music players. I know all of you like to listen to different types of music. Do you like to dance? Do you like to sing?"
Most of the students raised their hands as they all liked music. "I want to be a singer one day, to tell people about God that way," said Bjorg.
"Maybe you are called to the Mountain of Celebration," Miss Fitzgerald observed.
"I am so happy that I get to "Pray through the Seven Mountains" with you. I want you all to see what God has to say about the Seven Mountains. Over the next little while, you will get to look at 35 different people and see how God is using them to be world changers. Most importantly, you will get the opportunity to pray for them to be more like Jesus. You will also pray for God to give you help from Heaven to be a world changer."
Miss Fitzgerald was quiet for a minute, looking at every student one by one. "I have something important to tell you. You can make a big difference in the world, and Heaven wants to help you "Pray through the Seven Mountains."

The students looked at each other as if they shared a wonderful secret. They were excited at the idea of making a difference in the world and growing up to be a world changer.

"Now, everyone turn in your textbooks to page 14. We will begin to pray through the Mountain of Education….

*The "Mountain of Education" illustrations were completed using acrylic paint on canvas paper. These illustrations were painted in the perspective of a child with intended humor and cartoon appeal because learning is fun and takes imagination.

Mountain of Education

"Teach me good discernment and knowledge, for I believe in Your commandments" (Psalm 119:66).

Heaven's Thoughts:

The Mountain of Education is such a wonderful place. It is where dreams begin to come true. Education is where people can learn about the knowledge of God. They learn about creation, the stars in the sky, and butterflies. Through education, people can learn to love God and others. Education is very important for a city and a nation to be healthy. God cares so much about education. He desires for us to grow in education in every possible way. He will educate the cities and nations through counselors, teachers and pastors. Those cities will not pass away because they have been given the knowledge of God. Let the guidance flow. Let the instruction flow. Let the Mountain of Education grow.

Let's Pray Together:

Thank you, Lord, for the Mountain of Education. Thank you for teachers that tell people the truth, and show their students how truth can set people free. Thank you for the ability to learn from so many amazing people. Let me see you in education, Lord. The world needs education. I love when I read at home and learn about life. Lord, bless everyone who is in education. Give them a big kiss and let them know that you love them. Hold their hand and guide them, Jesus. Help me to learn wisdom and truth, and to be like the best teacher I can imagine. I love you, Jesus. Amen.

Welcome Five People in the Mountain of Education

(These five people are a sample of many)

Teacher
Librarian
Principal
School Counselor
Coach

Professor

"Teach me to do Your will, for You are my God; let Your good Spirit lead me on level ground" (Psalm 143:10).

Heaven's Thoughts:

Godly Teachers are wonderful people. They spend a majority of their life teaching people how to please God. Teachers are always available to help and they love to serve others. God, you bring so much encouragement through Teachers. Their positive attitudes can make such a lasting difference in the lives of their students. They love to share about any knowledge of you, how to live, how plants grow, how to love our family members. Teachers are so precious and wonderful. They would give everything to see their student succeed. Jesus, you are the master Teacher. All Teachers get their good ideas from you.

Let's Pray Together:

Thank you, Lord, for Teachers. They have so much love for their students. Without them, no one would know what to do; through them, their students can come to find the keys to life. Thank you for teachers who encourage me, who lift my head up when I am stuck on a school problem. I love how you give me precious jewels of wisdom through my Teachers. Thank you, Lord, for also bringing comfort through my Teachers. Jesus, I accept the Teachers that are in my life. I ask you to show them your kingdom thoughts. Give them a heart of love through education. Help me love them and appreciate them and be like them. I love you, Jesus. Amen.

Librarian

"And by knowledge the rooms are filled with all precious and pleasant riches" (Proverbs 24:4).

Heaven's Thoughts:

Librarians are such amazing people. They gather the story of humanity and make it available for all to see. They can be collectors of wisdom and keepers of your word. Even though all the books in the world could not contain the things that you have done for us, librarians still try to gather and contain so much of it. They hold on to books of treasure for the world. We have the Bible today because of them. We have educational tools today because of them. They put "His story" on display – history. They care for every little detail. They love to capture fantasy and creativity. They can be great distributors of your books and stories.

Let's Pray Together:

Thank you, Lord, for Librarians. You sent them here to preserve and share your testimony. They serve my school and library so well. I love how Librarians are very organized and know where every book is located. They are forever students of history. Thank you, Lord, for teaching me about creativity and art through the collections in the library. The library is a fun place to learn. I want to be educated with everything you have for me. You are a great God that loves to educate me. Thank you, Lord, that your heart is often shown in Librarians. Let them know how much they are loved. I love you, Jesus. Amen.

Principal

"Yes, I find delight in your rules; they give me guidance" (Psalm 119:24 NET).

Heaven's Thoughts:

Principals are often like our parents when we are at school. They care for the Lord's heart and plans. Principals can be like Jesus, when Jesus said, "They were Yours, You gave them to Me, and they have kept Your word" (John 17:6). Principals are gifted and entrusted with the Father's children. They have been given great responsibility to care for someone else's child. They are called by Heaven to show students the love of God and His plan for their lives. They can guide young people through life's lessons and trials. When they know and do what is right before the eyes of God, principles can lead people on paths of righteousness through life's rules and guidelines. They take great delight in bringing guidance from Heaven.

Let's Pray Together:

Thank you, Lord, for Principals. Jesus, I see how important they are. They care for me like my own parents. I love how they are always looking out for me. Thank you, Lord, for showing me guidance through my Principal. I know they give rules, but they are there to help me. Thank you, Lord, for putting such people in my life to help me succeed. I want to succeed in life with help from my Principal. Lord, bless my Principal. Help Principal to be faithful to teach people the way they should go. Help me to be more thankful of my Principal. I love you, Jesus. Amen.

School Counselor

"Where there is no guidance the people fall, but in abundance of counselors there is victory" (Proverbs 11:14).

Heaven's Thoughts:

The earth is filled with people that need help with their emotions, feelings, and path in life. This is what counselors are for. Counselors can gather wisdom from the heart of God and help put the person they are counseling on the correct path of life. People can get lost in life when counselors are not around. When counselors are around, they are able to help us find victory. They often have gifts of discernment and perception, to know what is possible in someone's life and future. They can come to know the desires of God's heart. Counselors help people through tough times and through happy times. They help to guide and educate us. They nurture us through our life to help us become the best person possible.

Let's Pray Together:

Thank you, Lord, for Counselors. Thank you for placing them my life and the lives of my friends and family. Counselors bring us encouragement, strength, and vision. Thank you, Jesus, for the great advice that comes from my counselors. I love how you are my guide through these wonderful people. You take my feet and place them on the path of life. My future and destiny is secure and true because of you, Jesus. Thank you, Lord, for the Counselors that help me with my future. I want to be more like my godly Counselors. Bless them in everything that they do. They are appreciated more than they know. I love you, Jesus. Amen.

Coach

"I press on toward the goal for the prize of the upward call of God in Christ Jesus" (Philippines 3:14).

Heaven's Thoughts:

Coaches plant the seeds of life in every generation. They can help raise children to become great leaders. They are often known as ultimate encouragers of fun. They make a way for people to have fun while learning. Coaches want everyone to become great in life and to be the best player in all sports. They help us win on the field and off the field. Coaches can lead people to win the upward call of God. They push us to be stronger and faster and smarter, so that we can win the prize. They teach us to work together and to accomplish our goals. They show us the importance of teamwork.

Let's Pray Together:

Thank you, Lord, for Coaches. They are a gift from the playgrounds of Heaven. I love to play on a team wanting to win first place. Thank you, Lord, for creating these possibilities in life. It is so much fun to play with my friends and score a goal.
Thank you for how I am being educated even when I am playing sports. I learn about you in new ways every day, Jesus. You teach me to love, to work, and to win. Those are all from you. Bless my Coaches. Let them know that they are the ultimate encouragers. Help me to be more like my coach.
I love you, Jesus. Amen.

GOVERNMENT

*The Mountain of Government illustrations were completed using watercolor on water paper. These illustrations were painted in landscape format because of their wide-ranging impact on society; they also focus on the community workforce rather than the individual.

Mountain of Government

"For a child will be born to us, a son will be given to us; And the government will rest on His shoulders; and His name will be called Wonderful Counselor, Mighty God, Eternal Father, Prince of Peace. There will be no end to the increase of His government or of peace" (Isaiah 9:6-7).

Heaven's Thoughts:

Government was God's idea. He rules Heaven with righteousness and justice. God also wants His perfect Government to be on the earth. That Government would rest on the shoulders of men and women who care about righteousness and justice, men and women in Government that have peace flowing like a river from the heart. These leaders make new guidelines and laws to protect us like a father would. They counsel people back to life through truth and love. There will be no end to the increase of God's Government and one day the whole world will be under His righteous governance forever.

Let's Pray Together:

Thank you, Lord, for the Mountain of Government. I want to see your perfect Government in my country – a Government filled with peace, righteousness and justice. You have always been so good to us through our Government leaders. Lord, give every country leaders that love freedom and peace. Thank you, Lord, for caring about our Government. Thank you for all of our Government workers. They help so many people. Thank you for the brave servants like firefighters, police officers and the military. I want to stand for freedom and peace like they do. I love you, Jesus. Amen.

Welcome Five People in the Mountain of Government

(These five people are a sample of many.)

Lawmakers
Administrative Assistants
Presidents
Firefighters
Navy

Lawmakers

"Is the Law then contrary to the promises of God? May it never be!" (Galatians 3:21)

Heaven's Thoughts:

Lawmakers can help to make freedom available through the Government. They care for people's hearts and they desire to provide the best possible life for everyone. Lawmakers are called to establish heavenly laws with righteousness and justice. They often have a gift for helping people. Their job is to never stop thinking about making the world a better place. Lawmakers protect and serve everyone who is under the government. They can help create good laws that bring back the beauty of the land and the people.

Let's Pray Together:

Thank you, Lord, for Lawmakers. Lawmakers that care for your heart make peace possible and they make a way for your promises to come true. I love the freedom that you have given my family in this country. Lord, you keep us safe because of righteous lawmakers. Thank you, Lord, for everything that I am able to do because of my freedom. I get to dream, grow up and become anyone I want, and live anywhere that I want. Thank you, Lord, for laws that come from the promises of God. Thank you for protecting the vulnerable little children through heavenly laws. Bless all of our lawmakers and help them to make laws from your heart. I love you, Jesus. Amen.

Administrative Assistants

"The law of the Lord is perfect, restoring the soul; the testimony of the Lord is sure, making wise the simple" (Psalm 19:7).

Heaven's Thoughts:

Administrative Assistants aid in bringing structure to the world. They have the ability to carry peace through their faithful assistance. When they desire to see the perfect will of God accomplished, they excel at co-laboring with God. Administrative Assistants can help Jesus, just like the Holy Spirit does. They help gather the fruit of good work. These Administrative Assistants take the difficult things of the world and make them simple. They are often gifted in bringing creativity to a job and making life easier for everyone else. They are a big reason we have success in our cities. They bring victories day in and day out even through routine tasks. Without them, the Mountain of Government wouldn't be healthy. They are such a blessing.

Let's Pray Together:

Thank you, Lord, for Administrative Assistants in the Mountain of Government. They are very helpful and caring as they bring assistance to everyone. Thank you, Lord, for these wonderful people that desire to serve you and do your will. They are some of the best helpers on the earth. There are administrative helpers everywhere because they are so important. Thank you, Lord, for these helpers that are like Elisha in the Bible, who washed the hands of Elijah. They help the person in charge to succeed. Lord, bless every of these Administrative Assistants and show them how much they are loved and cared for. Help me become a perfect Administrative Assistant to you. I love you, Jesus. Amen.

President

"Every person is to be in subjection to the governing authorities. For there is no authority except from God, and those which exist are established by God" (Romans 13:1).

Heaven's Thoughts:

The position of Presidents, Kings, and Rulers is ordained by God. There always needs to be someone in charge. Every city, state, and country is meant to love God and be good to Him. We are supposed to take care of the earth and give it to Jesus as a gift. The President has the power to help create cities that love God well. Heaven is in full support of godly Presidents and Kings. They make future plans for the country. They are meant to lead their people on a path of caring for others. They care about everyone and protect and serve them. These leaders are the beginning of a successful country. Presidents are to care for the heartbeat of their country. They are great people with great responsibility.

Let's Pray Together:

Thank you, Lord, for our nations' Presidents. They are a gift from you. You said in Scripture that we are to pray for our leaders every day. They have a big job in caring for the people that you have given them. They are strong and courageous leaders that care for my family. They can lead us and guide us from heaven with your help, Jesus. Thank you, Lord, that our President works every day for us to have a better life. Bless our President, keep him safe, and give him your heart for our country. Help me to be like a godly President, to lead and guide people into caring for what is right. I love you, Jesus. Amen.

Firefighter

"He delivers and rescues and performs signs and wonders in heaven and on earth" (Daniel 6:27).

Heaven's Thoughts:

Firefighters are willing to give their lives to save another. They rescue and protect people from harm. Everyday, they bring miracles of salvation to people's lives. Firefighters help rescue people from storms and fires. Firefighters are so important in the Mountain of Government because they rescue and save those things that we love. They are a blessing from Heaven when they help people in harm. When they save a life, it is a gift that God gave those people. Firefighters are responsible to make sure that we are all safe.

Let's Pray Together:

Thank you, Lord, for Firefighters. They create miracles every day. Lord, thank you for the love that they have and how they protect us. Thank you for the heroes that you have made them to be. People might not know them, but we know that they are here to save us, just like you are, Jesus. They have a gift for preserving life. I love how Firefighters are so courageous. Help me to be strong just like Firefighters. Help me to protect my family and my friends. I want to be a faithful hero every day. Bless them and keep them protected. I love you, Jesus. Amen.

Navy

"The Lord will protect him and keep him alive, and he shall be called blessed upon the earth; and do not give him over to the desire of his enemies" (Psalm 41:2).

Heaven's Thoughts:

Navy men and women serve their country at home, but many of them serve away from their families. They have grace to protect their families and country from harm. Heaven gives them strength to protect and serve in new ways every day. They sacrifice so that everyone else can live a good life. Heaven calls them "blessed upon the earth." With every ounce of strength they have, they fight so that our enemies will not succeed. The faithful men and women of the Navy and other Military Branches watch out for our country.

Let's Pray Together:

Thank you, Lord, for the men and women of all of our Military Branches. They have strength to stand up for what they believe in, just like you do. Thank you, Lord, that they desire to protect and serve us. They are blessed on the earth according to you. We love them, and we love what they do because they keep us safe from our enemies. Lord, show me how you protect me every day. Help me to serve others just as the Navy serves us. Help me be strong just as they are strong. Watch over them and take care of them when they are gone. Bless every one of them with your love. I love you, Jesus. Amen.

*The Mountain of Religion illustrations were completed with many complementary parts. The composition used is intended to capture moments in the Bible using a stained glass window. Windows are a symbolic picture in this Mountain because we are to have light shine through us also.

Mountain of Religion

"And He gave some as apostles, and some as prophets, and some as evangelists, and some as pastors and teachers, for the equipping of the saints for the work of service, to the building up of the body of Christ" (Ephesians 4:11-12).

Heaven's Thoughts:

Heaven's plan is that these five people within the Mountain of Religion would build up the body of Christ. Each person is called by God to be very active every day in furthering the cause of Christ. They serve God in different ways and all are needed. Apostles give us the big picture of what God is doing and help guide the overall process. Prophets help us to hear the heart of God. Evangelists bring people together and tell them about Jesus. Pastors care for everyone as a mother bird would care for her chicks. Teachers help us to know the knowledge of God. Every one of them is so important. The only way to have healthy cities and nations is to have all of these people working together.

Let's Pray Together:

Thank you, Lord, for the Mountain of Religion. You care so much for your church. You have given gifts to the body of Christ. Those gifts are apostles, prophets, pastors, teachers, and evangelists. They all desire to help people come to know who you are and to build up the body of Christ. Thank you, Lord, that each one is such a blessing. Lord, I ask that you would let the knowledge of Heaven fill the earth through the Mountain of Religion. Help everyone know your true heart through these people. "To Him be the glory in the church and in Christ Jesus to all generations forever and ever" (Ephesians 3:21). I love you, Jesus. Amen.

Welcome Five People in the Mountain of Religion

Pastor
Evangelist
Prophet
Teacher
Apostle

Pastor

"I am the good shepherd; the good shepherd lays down His life for the sheep" (John 10:11).

Heaven's Thoughts:

Pastors are some of the most caring people on earth. Their hearts are turned toward the lost and their desire is to bring spiritual health to every family through the saving knowledge of Jesus. They are like the "good Shepherd" that cares for the sheep and protects them. They are called to nurture and love people no matter what the situation may be. Pastors are so needed on the earth because people need tender love and care. When they care for the broken, hungry, wounded and needy, the earth can grow to be a blessed place.

Let's Pray Together:

Thank you, Lord, for Pastors. They are an amazing part of the body of Christ. Thank you for their tireless support of all things good. Pastors love God and others so much that they would even lay down their life for another. I love how they serve me every week at church and when they lead me to the knowledge of who you are, Jesus. I love that they never stop caring. Bless my Pastor and everyone who has a pastoral heart, even if no one knows them. Encourage my Pastor with thanksgiving and love from heaven. Help me to be more like you, Jesus, the ultimate Pastor. I want to be a good shepherd to my friends and family. I love you, Jesus. Amen.

Evangelist

"The gospel must first be preached to all the nations" (Mark 13:10).

Heaven's Thoughts:

Evangelists are put on the earth to reveal the story of Jesus to all people. Their one and only desire should be to tell people about Jesus so that others will be saved. Evangelists live their life helping others know the true knowledge of God. Evangelists gather truths from the Bible and share those truths to those that they meet. Heaven loves to partner with Evangelists because it is God's heart that no one would be lost. Evangelists are creative in showing the world the nature of God. There are Evangelists in every area of life. Heaven wants the knowledge of God on every Mountain.

Let's Pray Together:

Thank you, Lord, for Evangelists. There are, even now, Evangelists leading mission trips around the world. They care for the poor and the needy. Thank you, Lord, that they bring a cold cup of water to someone who is thirsty. They invite people into your everlasting kingdom every day. You love when people are invited in. Help me to invite you in to my life more and to help others invite you in to their heart and life. Bless the Evangelists that are in my life. Bless those who lead others into salvation. I pray that you would release more Evangelists into the earth. I love you, Jesus. Amen.

Prophet

"The prophet who prophesies of peace, when the word of the prophet comes to pass, then that prophet will be known as one whom the Lord has truly sent" (Jeremiah 28:9).

Heaven's Thoughts:

A prophet is a person who listens to the heart of God. Prophets are called to speak words of peace that come straight from the heart of God. They can bring Heaven's plans to God's people. When they speak the good and pure from Heaven to the earth, prophets help speak life and future into the children of God. They share stories from the Lord's heart. They are amazing people because they desire to hear and speak the word of God every day. Prophets dream of good things for their city and nation. They are dreamers because they can see what is possible in the future and help make it come to pass today.

Let's Pray Together:

Thank you, Lord, for Prophets. They are always trying to hear the voice of God for me and my family. Thank you for these amazing people that spend most of their life searching for your voice. I love prophets that look at your word and are excited to find the truth. I am blessed by prophets every day even if I don't know how much. Thank you, Lord, for prophetic voices in my life that speak to me truth, life, love and kindness. I am so blessed by people that speak peace and joy to me. Bless everyone that wants to hear the heart of God and speak it. Help me to hear your heart more clearly every day. Thank you for your wonderful voice. I love you, Jesus. Amen.

Teacher

"A pupil is not above his teacher; but everyone, after he has been fully trained, will be like his teacher" (Luke 6:40).

Heaven's Thoughts:

Teachers are sent from Heaven into every Mountain. They are ordained to help people learn about the knowledge of God in every area of life. They care about showing people the correct way to live. Teachers care for the heart of every individual in their area of influence and desire for them to have the best possible life. Teachers in church help others learn how to love. They help us to hear God. Teachers are nurturers; they are like fathers and mothers in the Mountain of Religion. Teachers can help people succeed. The earth is a blessed place because of Teachers.

Let's Pray Together:

Thank you, Lord, for Teachers in the Mountain of Religion. Thank you for those who believe in me and bring me the education that I need to serve God. They teach me to know more about you, Jesus. They also teach me about who I am in you. Most importantly, they teach me how to partner with you every day. Thank you for teachers in my church who show me how to love my family and friends. Teachers also show me how to have fun in loving God. Bless all the Teachers that are in my life. Help me to grow up like a heavenly Teacher. I want to help teach people about Jesus. I love you, Jesus. Amen.

Apostle

"Having been built on the foundation of the apostles and prophets, Christ Jesus Himself being the corner stone" (Ephesians 2:20).

Heaven's Thoughts:

Apostles are the foundation to the church. They help lead and guide those in the Mountain of Religion. Apostles want to see clearly from God for themselves and for everyone around them. They have a heart for restoration, justice and unity among everyone. Apostles are leaders who bring change in big ways through love, honor and servant-hood. These amazing men and women serve God in their church, city and state. Their desire is to do and say what God is doing in Heaven.

Let's Pray Together:

Thank you, Lord, for Apostles. They are selfless and humble, just like you. Thank you for how Apostles lead your people. Jesus, give them vision and direction to guide the body of Christ. Thank you for building healthy churches that care for your heart. I love it when I am able to grow at church because of Apostles. Lord, help my city and state walk in love, honor and servant-hood like Apostles do. I am so blessed to have godly Apostles in my life. Bless the people around me that seek to grow your church. Help me to have a heart for your plans, peace, and church. I love you, Jesus. Amen.

*The Mountain of Media illustrations were completed using a marker on plain paper, then transformed by photo editing software. These illustrations were planned around the movement and energy of media and pulled from real life examples.

Mountain of Media

"Finally, brothers and sisters, whatever is true, whatever is worthy of respect, whatever is just, whatever is pure, whatever is lovely, whatever is commendable, if something is excellent or praiseworthy, think about these things" (Philippians 4:8).

Heaven's Thoughts:

The Mountain of Media has always been a leader in giving people news. The Bible says, "Love is to do good and communicate" (Hebrews 13:16). The Mountain of Media can give truth to all generations. Through the Mountain of Media, many are able hear the story of creation, life, and humanity. Media works with all of the other Mountains and communicates about everything. The Mountain of Media is the communication piece that reaches to the ends of the earth through written and spoken broadcasting.

Let's Pray Together:

Thank you, Lord, for the Mountain of Media. This Mountain has the ability to communicate to everyone about who you are and what you have done. I love to watch my favorite shows on TV and to hear news that makes me happy and hopeful. Thank you, Lord, for people who speak of your love and life through the Mountain of Media. Thank you for the education that is communicated in this Mountain. Lord, send more people to be in this Mountain that have a hopeful heart and voice for what you are doing. Help me to communicate your story just like the Mountain of Media does everyday. I love you, Jesus. Amen.
Welcome Five People in the Mountain of Media

Welcome Five People in the Mountain of Media

(The five people are just a sample of many)
Reporter
Writer
Director
Radio Host
News Anchor

Reporter

"It was a true report which I heard in my own land about your words and your wisdom" (1 Kings 10:6).

Heaven's Thoughts:

Reporters give information about what happens to people all over the world. They can report breaking news in a hopeful and caring way. When they want to see the truth in every person and situation, reporters search out the truth and expose things that are bad. Reporters work with the other Mountains and speak a true report from which they have heard. Reporters are called by God to servants at heart by desiring to see the bad things of the world come to an end through their voice.

Let's Pray Together:

Thank you, Lord, for Reporters. They can be a mouthpiece to all of the Mountains by communicating good things to everyone in the world. Some Reporters are on TV and some are behind a computer, but they are all meant to uncover the hidden truths of life and your word. Thank you, Lord, for putting people on the earth that desire to find truth even when it is hidden. I love when my family gets to know about life in our city and country through good reporters. Bless all the Reporters that we can depend on when we turn on the news. Help me to speak good things that help the people around me. I love you, Jesus. Amen.

Writers

"Then behold, the man clothed in linen at whose loins was the writing case reported, saying, 'I have done just as You have commanded me'" (Ezekiel 9:11).

Heaven's Thoughts:

Writers tell the story of life through words. Writers that come from Heaven have been around since the beginning of time. Writers like to journal about the things that God has done. They desire to share their creative imagination with others by telling wonderful and unique stories. People are happy when they read stories that bring hope and life. The story of Jesus was given to many writers so that it may be told to everyone in the world. Heaven loves Writers because they have the power to change the world through passionate writing.

Let's Pray Together:

Thank you, Lord, for Writers. They make your heart known through creative writing. I love Writers because I love to read all different kinds of stories. I get to read about my favorite heroes and Bible characters. Thank you for educating me through Writers at school. Jesus, even you had writers around you that kept your precious words. Bless all the writers that keep your words and record your truth. Lord, give them an imagination from Heaven to tell beautiful stories. Jesus, help me to be an amazing Writer for you. Thank you for words that change my life. I love you, Jesus. Amen.

Director

For the music director; a psalm of David.

"The heavens declare the glory of God; the sky displays his handiwork" (Psalm 19:1).

Heaven's Thoughts:

Directors help direct the Mountain of Media. They direct music, movies, TV shows, writing projects, and other things too. Directors are responsible for creating and planning media projects. As the Father directed and created the heavens and the earth, directors can share God's heart in the Mountain of Media. They can take a vision and help make it piece of art. Directors have an understanding of leadership and teamwork. Directors try their best to create beautiful images that they can share with the world. We are blessed because of directors.

Let's Pray Together:

Thank you, Lord, for directors. King David had a director of music who helped him to sing about the glory of God and the creation of Heaven. We are blessed to have people that care about beauty and truth in the Mountain of Media. Thank you, Lord, for the Directors of my favorite shows and movies. I love when Directors can find inspiration from you that is fun and creative. Bless every one of the Directors in the Mountain of Media and help them to have vision from Heaven. Help me to direct my life, to take your word and shine it all around. Help me to also become a visionary for what you are doing. I love you, Jesus. Amen.

Radio Host

"How you have advised the one without wisdom, and abundantly revealed your insight" (Job 26:3).

Heaven's Thoughts:

Radio Hosts have the ability to share about who God is on talk shows and radio shows. They are often encouragers at heart and love to make people happy with good news. They can bring joy and laughter to our day through stories of love and excitement. Radio Hosts also release wonderful music from different singers and bands – music that inspires us, brings us peace, and makes us want to have fun. Radio Hosts can also teach us wisdom to help us have a better life. Even though we can't always see them, they are there encouraging us along the way.

Let's Pray Together:

Thank you, Lord, for Radio Hosts that share inspirational stories that connect people to their community. I love to turn on the radio in the car and hear wonderful advice and music that makes me happy. I enjoy my favorite music and I love to learn about what is going on in the world through the radio. Thank you, Lord, for people who care for your knowledge and truth throughout the world. Thank you for the encouragement that I receive on the radio. Bless every one of the Radio Hosts in my city and help them to speak truth and encouragement just like you do, Jesus. Help me to communicate your word like godly Radio Hosts do. I love you, Jesus. Amen.

News Anchor

"There they continued to proclaim the good news" (Acts 14:7).

Heaven's Thoughts:

News Anchors are on the front lines of releasing news to the world. They are the face of the Mountain of Media. They can also be messengers for the Kingdom of God in Media. News Anchors are gifted communicators and thoughtful people. It is wonderful when News Anchors desire to share uplifting and heartfelt stories and when they speak justice and truth and tell stories of tremendous courage. We are informed by their breaking news and we are encouraged by their loving hearts.

Let's Pray Together:

Thank you, Lord, for News Anchors. We are truly blessed by their gifts of communication. Every day they speak truth and justice on the TV to inform us about life and how to live it better. They also tell us how to stay safe when there are storms outside. Thank you, Lord, for News Anchors that care for me and my family. I love when my family watches helpful and hopeful news. Bless all the News Anchors in my city and nation. Inspire more heavenly communicators to speak your word on TV. Help me also to speak truth every day with my friends and family. I love you, Jesus. Amen.

$Economy$

*The Mountain of Economy illustrations are a collage of images with bright washes behind the pencil drawings. These illustrations were designed to portray all the facets of the Personal Representative through printed examples that promote areas of interest in their lives.

Mountain of Economy

"He summoned ten of his servants, gave them ten minas, and said to them, 'Do business with these until I come back'" (Luke 19:13).

Heaven's Thoughts:

The Mountain of Economy encompasses areas such as businesses, banks and money. These businesses and people are often visionaries who are hopeful about the future. The Mountain of Economy is an important place for giving money to those in need. Heaven loves to partner with companies to provide jobs for families. Money that is created in the Mountain of Economy can be used to help many people and save many lives. The Mountain of Economy helps a country grow and creates opportunities for the future.

Let's Pray Together:

Thank you, Lord, for the Mountain of Economy. This is a wonderful group of people that desire to build and expand wealth for their family and city. Thank you for the ones who have a humble heart and serve the people around them through providing goods and services. Thank you, Lord, for the honesty and hard work that is shown in the Mountain of Economy. I love when I am able to go into a store and buy gifts for my friends and family. Bless each and everyone that is in the Mountain of Economy and help them to be smart with money. Help me to be a cheerful giver and build wealth with you. I love you, Jesus. Amen.

Welcome Five People in the Mountain of Economy

(The five people are just a sample of many)

Construction Worker

Business Owner

Bank Worker

Hair Stylist

Chef

Construction Worker

"According to all that I am showing you, the pattern of the tabernacle and the pattern of all its furnishings, you must make it exactly so" (Exodus 25:9).

Heaven's Thoughts:

Construction Workers build foundations for good homes and businesses. They are hard workers that care for their families. They are very focused at work and want to build things the right way. Construction Workers are very creative and ready to work on any type of project. Every house in your neighborhood and every building you see in your city were built by Construction Workers. Construction Workers ordained by Heaven are trustworthy and reliable. They are great workers.

Let's Pray Together:

Thank you, Lord, for Construction Workers. They build homes and businesses for people to have a safe and comfortable life. They build homes for people who don't have homes and fix broken or old homes. They are ready and willing to serve everyone. I love when I'm able to go home and relax and feel safe. Thank you, Lord, for Construction Workers and how they bring strength and security to my city. Bless every Construction Worker in my neighborhood and let them know that they are loved and cared for. Help me to be a trustworthy and reliable friend like they are. I love you, Jesus. Amen.

Business Owner

"He gathered these together, along with the workmen in similar trades, and said, 'Men, you know that our prosperity comes from this business'" (Acts 19:25).

Heaven's Thoughts:

Business Owners provide goods and services to make everyone's life easier. They are very important for a healthy economy. Business Owners are meant to be focused and passionate about the vision that God has given them for their business. They are able to help many people at the same time. Skilled men and women partner with God when they create ways to help people live better lives. Business Owners can help make all of the Mountains successful. Heaven loves godly Business Owners because they care about their city and nation – Business Owners who love to give money and gifts to people in need.

Let's Pray Together:

Thank you, Lord, for Business Owners who search out the needs of a community and provide food, technology, and other helpful things. Business Owners are so creative. Thank you, Lord, for all the businesses in my area. Thank you for how they change my life and make it easier. I am so blessed by Business Owners that care about the success of my family. Bless every one of the Business Owners in my city and give them smart ideas on how to prosper. Help me to live my life to be great at many things like Business Owners are. I love you, Jesus. Amen.

Bank Worker

"That I may cause those who love me to inherit wealth, and that I may fill their treasuries" (Proverbs 8:21).

Heaven's Thoughts:

Bank Workers are good at taking care of other people's resources. They put people's money in a safe place for security. Bank Workers help people send money all around the world. They partner with people to make more money through their bank. They are ordained to be caring people that desire success for everyone that they meet. Bank Workers are honest and trustworthy with money. They help people plan their future and give them advice on how to save money and make money.

Let's Pray Together:

Thank you, Lord, for Bank Workers. They are good at watching over resources from Heaven. Thank you that Bank Workers help to keep my family's money in a safe place. Bank Workers are so helpful when my family wants to buy groceries and gifts. They provide my family with money to buy a house or a car. We are blessed to have trustworthy people care for our hard-earned money. Bless all of the Bank Workers in my city and show them ways to make more money. Lord, help me to be smart with all of the money that you give me. I love you, Jesus. Amen.

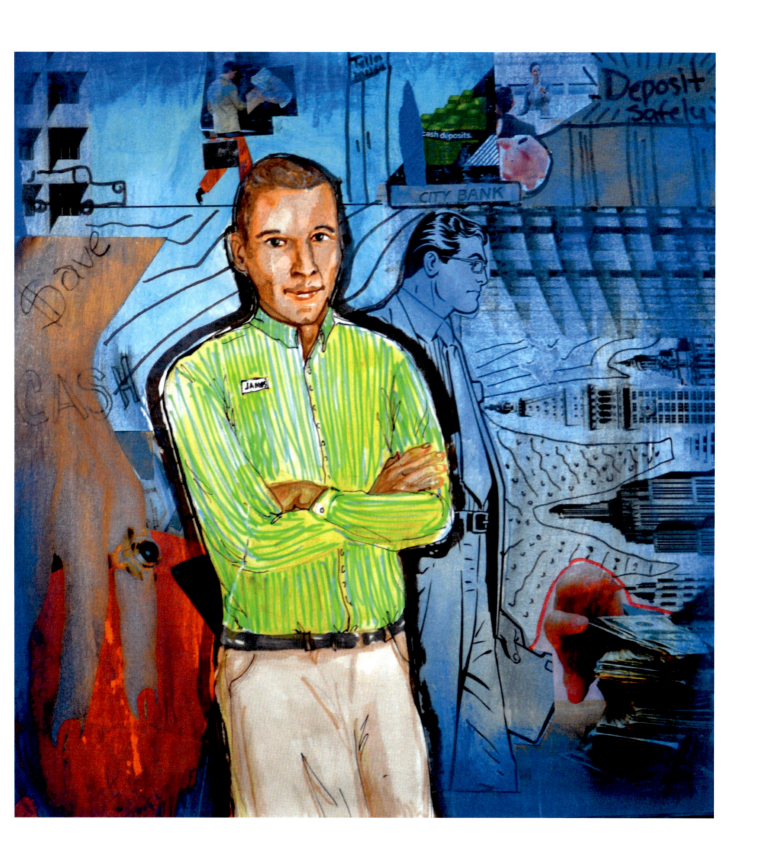

Hair Stylist

"Moses summoned every skilled person in whom the Lord had put skill, everyone whose heart stirred him to volunteer to do the work" (Exodus 36:2).

Heaven's Thoughts:

Hair Stylists are very hard workers and some of the most creative people on the planet. They can be understanding people who love to listen to the hearts of everyone that they serve. Hair Stylists are often visionaries that create beauty for individuals. They are faithful to their customers and are friendly people to be around. Hair Stylists can also be in the Mountain of Celebration because they create beauty around the world. They usually give great advice while cutting your hair.

Let's Pray Together:

Thank you, Lord, for Hair Stylists. They are faithful and true to all of their customers. My family members often get their hair cut by Hair Stylists who are so good at serving and loving my family. I love when I get a new haircut because it makes me look amazing. Thank you, Lord, for Hair Stylists and how they bring out the beauty in everyone. The world would be boring if everyone had the same haircut. Bless every Hair Stylist in my city and help them to be prosperous and creative. Help me to learn how to help people and take care of them like Hair Stylists do. I love you, Jesus. Amen.

Chef

"To the one who gives food to all living things, for his loyal love endures" (Psalm 136:25).

Heaven's Thoughts:

Chefs prepare wonderful food so that we can be fed and amazed by their recipes. Chefs work very hard so that we can experience food from all the over the world. They have a heart for health and wholeness. Heavenly chefs care about the earth and care about the food that goes into our bodies. They know what it means to taste and see that the Lord is good. Chefs can also change the culture of a city by providing excellence and healthy dishes. They are generous and release life through the food they provide.

Let's Pray Together:

Thank you, Lord, for Chefs. They make many people happy with their recipes and dishes. Food is so important to survival and it also brings pleasure in life. Lord, you call yourself the Bread of Life. You love food and so do I. Thank you for Chefs who work hard to prepare meals for people they don't even know. I am so blessed to have amazing food that is grown in gardens all around us. Thank you for all of my favorite foods. Bless every one of the Chefs in my neighborhood and help them create healthy works of art. Help me to also provide tasty food for my family as I get older. I love you, Jesus. Amen.

*The Mountain of Family illustrations were completed using watercolor. These illustrations were designed around a framed portrait that you might find in your own home. The focus of the illustrations is to capture a moment of life with a camera or a sketch.

Mountain of Family

"Not one of the Lord's faithful promises to the family of Israel was left unfulfilled; every one was realized" (Joshua 21:45 NET).

Heaven's Thoughts:

Every Mountain begins with the Mountain of Family. It is the start of life and love. Everyone in the Mountain of Family is strengthened by love. In the Mountain of Family you will find protection, care, and encouragement. Heaven loves the Mountain of Family and desires to see it grow and be healthy. A good relationship is a beautiful thing that is highly desired in heaven. The Mountain of Family is a place where everyone loves to be with one another. You are safe and cared for in the Mountain of Family.

Let's Pray Together:

Thank you, Lord, for the Mountain of Family. Family is so important for a healthy life. God, through the Mountain of Family I come to understand that you want to have a relationship with me. Family is all about connecting with people that you love. Thank you, Lord, for amazing family members that care for my success every day. Thank you for my parents and how they care for me so much. I love to come home and feel loved and appreciated by my family. Family was your idea, Jesus. We are so blessed to have families. Bless my family and my friend's families. Help me to be a good family member from heaven. I love you, Jesus. Amen.

Welcome Five People in the Mountain of Family

(The five people are just a sample of many)

Father
Mother
Nurse
Social Worker
Nanny

Father

"If you keep My commandments, you will abide in My love; just as I have kept My Father's commandments and abide in His love" (John 15:10).

Heaven's Thoughts:

Fathers are ordained to be an image of our loving Father in Heaven. They have strong hearts and are faithful to their families. They love to serve and teach us everything they know. Fathers are such an important part of the family unit. Although they are strong, they are also meant to be kindhearted and to spread peace through feelings of security and acceptance. Fathers can bring out the best in their children. Fathers are so fun to be around and are needed in the family. Everyone has a Father in Heaven that loves and cares for them more than they know.

Let's Pray Together:

***If you do not have an active earthly Father, then pray to your heavenly Father.**

Thank you, Lord, for Fathers. Thank you for being my Father in Heaven, and thank you for my Father on earth and how he has cared for me and blessed me more than I know. Not everyone has a Father on earth. Lord, bring love and comfort to those who do not have an earthly Father. There is so much love that is given through Fathers. When I grow up I want to be just like a godly Father. I am so blessed to have a Father in Heaven that supports me. I love when I get to spend time with my Father and laugh and play. It makes me so happy to feel loved in that way. Bless my Father and release your love and appreciation over him. Help me to be the best child that I could be for my Father. I love you, Jesus. Amen.

Mother

"Honor your father and mother, and love your neighbor as yourself" (Matthew 19:19).

Heaven's Thoughts:

Mothers are the glue that holds the family together. They are nurturing from the moment a child is born. Mothers are very understanding of their children's needs and desires. They desire to see their children full of happiness and life. A mother with a heavenly perspective is caring, affectionate, and supportive of her children. Mothers are a great picture of the love that we receive from Heaven. Mary, mother of Jesus, believed in Jesus' greatness before anyone else did. Mary saw hope and love in her child's future and she prepared Him for greatness.

Let's Pray Together:

***If you do not have an active earthly Mother, you can pray to the Holy Spirit.**

Thank you, Lord, for Mothers. They are such a blessing every day. I love it when my Mother gives me love and affection; it makes me feel happy and secure. Thank you for my Mother who works so hard for me and my family. I am so blessed by her ability to care and teach me every day. Lord, help me to never forget how much my Mother supports me and has fun with me. I am grateful that you blessed me with my Mother. Bless my Mother with heavenly appreciation for everything that she does for my family. Release love and peace to her. Help me to be like my mom, because she is amazing. I love you, Jesus. Amen.

Nurse

"For I will restore you to health and I will heal you of your wounds,' declares the Lord" (Jeremiah 30:17).

Heaven's Thoughts:

Nurses often have special gifts of compassion and patience. They run towards problems to bring health and wholeness to those in pain and need. Nurses are very hard workers that choose to put others before themselves. They have a heart for humanity and they carry wisdom that brings life. They can partner with Jesus on a daily basis to restore people to health through healing, miracles and medicine. Nurses are often compared to angels because they save many lives. Heaven loves Nurses because God wants everyone to be well.

Let's Pray Together:

Thank you, Lord, for Nurses. They serve people with love and compassion. Thank you that Nurses rescue and help those who are sick and in need. I love to feel protection and security in knowing that Nurses are there if I ever get sick. Nurses bring life to so many people. I am happy and thankful for every Nurse in the world because they make the world a better place. Bless them in everything they do and continue to show them your heart. Give them wisdom, courage and rest to be the best they can be. Help me to be as caring and smart as they are. I love you, Jesus.
Amen.

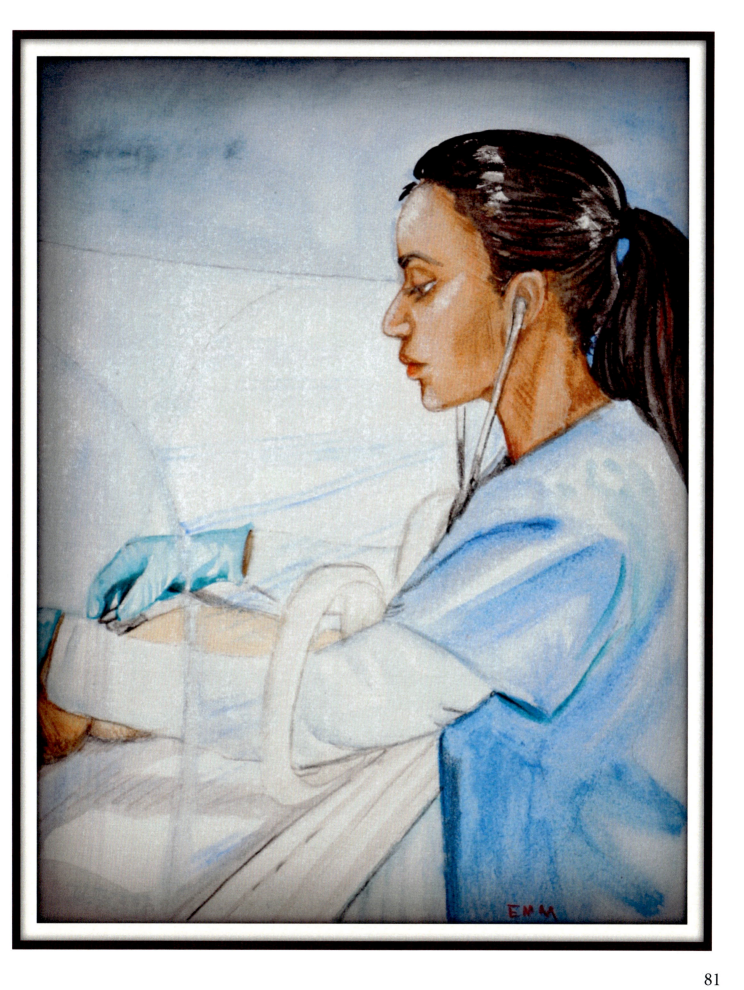

Social Worker

"The righteous is concerned for the rights of the poor, the wicked does not understand such concern" (Proverbs 29:7).

Heaven's Thoughts:

Social Workers care for the small and vulnerable children. They desire justice, freedom, and a wonderful life for every human. They devote their lives to place children in loving homes that care for their every need. Social Workers have hopeful eyes for everyone, no matter their circumstances. They believe the best is available for every child. Social Workers are called to be gracious and compassionate like Jesus. They care for children when no one else does. Social Workers are loved and adored from Heaven.

Let's Pray Together:

Thank you, Lord, for Social Workers who care for the rights of children that do not have families. They are such a blessing. Social Workers go above and beyond to make sure someone knows that they are valued and important. They bring a caring heart into many people's lives and I thank them for that. I am so appreciative that Social Workers are working in my city to bring a better life to so many people. I love how you, Jesus, do good through them even when it sometimes goes unnoticed. Bless the Social Workers in my city and give them a hug from Heaven for what they do. Help me to be gracious like they are. I love you, Jesus. Amen.

Nanny

"The Child continued to grow and become strong, increasing in wisdom; and the grace of God was upon Him" (Luke 2:40).

Heaven's Thoughts:

Nannies help watch and raise children that are not their own. They have the gift of helping others and a spirit of servant-hood. They can help train up a child in the way they should go. Nannies have a caring heart and are loving and kind to those they watch over. They have the responsibility to nurture children as a mother would nurture her own children. Nannies are often patient and are good teachers. Nannies help families to be more successful. Nannies assist families that have working parents. Heaven loves Nannies and we appreciate them for their hard work.

Let's Pray Together:

Thank you, Lord, for Nannies. They are very important to all families. Nannies care for children, including me. They are helpful to my parents when my parents are at work or busy. Thank you, Lord, for them when they come over to watch me. I love when I am able to play and have fun with my Nanny or babysitter. They help me grow up and become smarter and more loving. Lord, bless all of the Nannies and babysitters and let them know how much you appreciate them. Help me to love and honor my Nannies and babysitters more. I love how they take care of me. I love you, Jesus. Amen.

CELEBRATION

*The Mountain of Celebration illustrations were completed using a sculpted doll positioned in a staged or created background. These illustrations were built to inspire bigger possibilities through intended doll or action figure role playing.

Mountain of Celebration

"And David was dancing before the Lord with all his might, and David was wearing a linen ephod" (2 Samuel 6:14).

Heaven's Thoughts:

The Mountain of Celebration is the home of creativity and individual expression. There are singers and song writers that share about God. There are painters and sculptors that display the beauty of Heaven. The Mountain of Celebration is filled with life, laughter and joyful noises. The Mountain of Celebration is also home to all kinds of sports. Celebration is found in different types of artists all over the world. King David danced before the Lord and celebrated with God. Heaven loves worshipers that celebrate His goodness.

Let's Pray Together:

Thank you, Lord, for the Mountain of Celebration. It is a place where so many people can tell about the love that you have given them. Many people find you in the Mountain of Celebration because you make our lives like a party. I love to listen to wonderful music with my family. Thank you, Lord, for everyone who is in the Mountain of Celebration. I love hearing songs of joy and seeing dancers dance with the Lord. The Mountain of Celebration brings hope and life to everyone around the world. Help the Mountain of Celebration to be creative like Heaven and fun like Jesus. Help me to find celebration every day through you. I love you, Jesus. Amen.

Welcome Five People in the Mountain of Celebration

(The five people are just a sample of many)

Singer
Painter
Soccer Player
Dancer
Pianist

Singer

"Sing to the Lord a new song; sing to the Lord, all the earth" (Psalm 96:1).

Heaven's Thoughts:

Singers sing the sound of Heaven through different types of music. They sing to the Lord a new song and all the earth celebrates. Singers release heavenly emotion and love through their songs. Music touches our hopes and desires and encourages us to be the best person we can be. Singers release healing and wholeness through their soothing sounds. Everyone is a worshiper at heart and singers allow people to worship freely everywhere. Singers shout from the Mountaintops everything that the Lord has done.

Let's Pray Together:

Thank you, Lord, for Singers. They have such a wonderful gift that encourages everyone. I love when I listen to music and it makes me want to have fun with my friends and family. Thank you, Lord, that Singers and Songwriters give people an opportunity to celebrate. It is a wonderful thing to have so many Singers on the earth. Bless the worship leaders at my church and give them heavenly songs to sing. Bless every Singer on the radio to hear your voice in their music. Help me to always have a new song in my heart for you. I desire to love you through singing every day. I love you, Jesus. Amen.

Painter

"You alone are the Lord. You have made the heavens, the heaven of heavens with all their host, the earth and all that is on it, the seas and all that is in them. You give life to all of them, and the heavenly host bows down before You" (Nehemiah 9:6).

Heaven's Thoughts:

Painters are creative visionaries that have the ability to paint heavenly beauty onto a canvas. The Lord God is the creator of all things beautiful; painters capture what He has done. They are extremely talented and when they look to Heaven for inspiration, they bring life through their different types of art and paintings. Every day, God releases majestic art in the sky and on the earth. Painters can partner with God in telling the story of creation to people of all ages. They paint the world in a way that is remembered forever.

Let's Pray Together:

Thank you, Lord, for Painters. They are great at creating and capturing beauty from Heaven. Thank you for making such a beautiful planet that we get to look at every day. Painters tell your story to everyone through a paintbrush. I love to paint different pictures just like painters do. Thank you, Lord, that I can become a painter of beauty also. I love when my parents are happy with something that I have painted. Bless all the painters that paint love and hope to the world. Help me to be an excellent painter and to tell my story through the beauty of what you have done for me. I love you, Jesus. Amen.

Soccer Player

"Whatever you do, do all to the glory of God" (1 Corinthians 10:31).

Heaven's Thoughts:

Soccer Players are athletic and enjoy competing, playing as a team, and winning. Soccer Players fit in the Mountain of Celebration because they bring a lot of fun and excitement to those who watch the sport. Soccer Players are very strong and quick. They usually love to entertain and will do anything to see their team win. They show us what it means to "run the race to win the prize," which is something the Bible tells us to do. Soccer Players and other sports players show teamwork and unity. Playing a sport is good for our health and fun as well.

Let's Pray Together:

Thank you, Lord, for Soccer Players. When they play soccer for the glory of God, they can bring happiness to everyone that is watching. Thank you, Lord, for Soccer Players and other sports players because they show great teamwork. I love to play sports with my family and friends. I love when I am able to work on a team with them. It is so much fun to play together and "run the race to win the prize." Bless every Soccer Player and help them to play for You, Jesus. Give them strength and protect them as they play. Help me to play all my sports and games with love and teamwork. I love you, Jesus. Amen.

Dancer

"Let them praise His name with dancing..." (Psalm 149:3).

Heaven's Thoughts:

Dancers are a wonderful depiction of celebration in Heaven. They are flexible and creative in their dance styles. Dancers release creativity and beauty through each motion and gesture. They flow like the wind and sometimes dance like a drum. Dancers can release joy and happiness to everyone. They practice very hard so that they can show the audience an amazing show. Heaven loves when people use their body to glorify God. The Bible is filled with celebration and dance. Dancers can praise the Lord through their dance.

Let's Pray Together:

Thank you, Lord, for dancers. They are creative and so much fun. I love when I am able to dance and have fun with life. I want to dance and glorify You, God. Thank you, Lord, for dancers like King David. He poured out his heart and praised you with his dance. The Mountain of Celebration is filled with talented and spirit-filled dancers. Bless every Dancer that lives in my city and neighborhood. Help them to show the world your love and beauty. Help me to be joyful and dance to show you my praise. I want to dance for you. I love you, Jesus. Amen.

Pianist

"Along with their relatives, all of them trained and skilled in music for the Lord..." (1 Chronicles 25:7).

Heaven's Thoughts:

A Pianist is someone who plays the piano. Pianists are so skillful with this instrument that they can make wonderful music by moving their fingers. They show the power of God through their fingertips. Heaven is filled with wonderful noises like the piano. Pianists can open the Heavens with their melodies and release the love of God through beautiful music. Beautiful music from the piano is relaxing and moving. People who play the piano and other instruments give the world creative songs from Heaven.

Let's Pray Together:

Thank you, Lord, for people who play godly music. It is so much fun to dance and play with creative music from Heaven. Everyone who makes music has a beautiful talent that the world needs to know. Thank you for songs that make me happy and songs that give me peace. Help me to find your heart and love through different kinds of music. I want to hear wonderful music from Heaven. Thank you for all the people in my life that sing and play instruments. They are a blessing. Help me to be creative and make melodies with you. I love making music with you. I love you, Jesus. Amen.

Back to Class

Miss Fitzgerald closed the book and looked up at her students. "What did you think of the 7 Mountains book, everyone? Do you feel that God wants to help you become whoever you want to be?"

"Yes! Miss Fitzgerald" the students chorused enthusiastically.

"That is great news," answered their teacher. "I am so happy that I was able to take all of you through the Seven Mountains. As you learned, the Seven Mountains are for everyone. You can dream to become anyone that you want to be. God wants to help you bring His love to every area of the world. Do any of you know which Mountain you would like to live and work in when you grow up?"

Miss Fitzgerald looked at the student from South America. "Santiago, what Mountain would you liked to be in when you grow up and who would you like to become in that Mountain?"

Santiago cocked his head to one side, thinking for a minute before answering, "I would like to be in the Mountain of Education. I want to be a professor and help guide people to become the best person possible."

Everyone smiled. "Fantastic," Miss Fitzgerald answered. "What about you Zoey?"

"I would like to be in the Mountain of Government," Zoey replied. "I want to be a firefighter and help save lives."

"That is great news," the teacher responded. "How about you, Qiang? You mentioned that you might like to help people in Asia learn about Jesus."

Qiang nodded. "I would like to be in the Mountain of Economy. I want to be business owner and sell coffee from my café. I can play good music and offer books about Jesus as well."

"That is a very good idea, Qiang. What about you, Bjorg? What Mountain would you like to be in? Do you still want to be a singer?

"Yes, Miss Fitzgerald. I would like to be in the Mountain of Celebration. I can inspire people through the music I sing."

"Great, Bjorg. How about you, Emma? "I would like to be in the Mountain of Religion. I want to be an Evangelist and lead mission trips to every country," Emma answered with a smile.

"Very good, Emma. That would be an exciting thing." Miss Fitzgerald turned to Zoey. "And what would you like to do, Zoey?"

"I would like to be in the Mountain of Family. I want to be a Mother and write books about parenting. Then it would be like I was in two Mountains at the same time."

Miss Fitzgerald smiled. "That is a good point, Zoey, and that is a great choice as well. Omari, what about you? What Mountain would you like to be in?"

"I would like to be in the Mountain of Media. I want to be a director of movies in Hollywood."

"Wow! Miss Fitzgerald answered. "It is so encouraging that all of you want to be in at least one of the Mountains. I know that every one of you will do just great. It has been a wonderful year going through the Seven Mountains with you. I just want to say a few last things before you go home for the summer."

The students sat quietly as their teacher walked over to the window and looked outside for a moment. She turned to her class again and spoke with enthusiasm.

"Every one of you is gifted in so many ways. I loved being with you all year. I am so excited about your future because I know that you can do anything you set your mind and heart to. I know that you will grow up to become amazing men and women. You will help many people along the way. You will even save lives. Every one of you has a hopeful perspective about your future and because of that, you can change the world. I know that you will change the world because you are …"

"World changers!" The fifth graders chorused.

"That's right," Miss Fitzgerald smiled. "Remember, you are children with purpose, and God is your partner. Class, you are dismissed!! Don't forget to hug your teacher before you go."

Everyone ran to give Miss Fitzgerald a big hug. They knew it would be a wonderful summer. They knew it would be a wonderful life.

Glossary

A Blessing/To Bless – To make someone else's life happy, joyous, and full. To bless means to provide for another person's needs no matter what the situation is. Blessings also come from God and are similar to God's "gifts."

A Hero – Someone who acts with bravery and courage to save someone or something. A hero is a very loving person and wants to help people in need or in danger.

Administrative Assistants – People who give administrative and support to an office or organization to help it run smoothly and operate well. They bring help and structure to the world by taking on very hard tasks and making them simple. Our government is healthy because of administrative assistants.

Advice – Kind words of guidance and comfort that help people when they are struggling with a difficult time. Advice helps people make good decisions.

Affectionate – To be loving, tender and caring.

Angels – Heavenly beings that help God watch over you and guide you to make the right choices.

Apostle – One who is sent on a mission. They give us the big picture of what God is doing. They love others with sincere hearts and can perform miracles. They have a special message from Jesus to tell the world of all that God is doing!

Appreciation – Being thankful for someone or something; having a thankful heart for all of the blessings God has provided in your life.

Assistance – To give help to or get help from another person. It is okay to ask for assistance when you are struggling. There are plenty of people around you who love to give you help.

Athletic – Physically active and strong. Someone who enjoys playing sports and is good at it. Someone who loves to compete and has fun doing it. Soccer players are an example of people who are athletic.

Bank Worker/Banker – A person employed by a bank. These people are good at taking care of other people's resources. They put people's money in a safe place for security. They help people plan their future and give advice on how to save money.

Banks – A place where money is stored for safekeeping. Bankers work at banks.

Bible – A very special book written by God's Spirit through men on earth. The Bible gives us a glimpse of what it means to love God and one another. The Bible tells people that Jesus is the way to Heaven and the key to living a happy and purposed life on earth.

Body of Christ – You and your family and those that love Jesus are the body of Christ. The body of Christ believes that Jesus is the Son of God and work to serve God in different ways.

Brave/Bravery – Fearless, not afraid of doing something. Doing the right thing even when it may seem hard. You can ask God for bravery and He will strengthen you to do tasks that seem too hard to do on your own.

Bread of Life – A name for Jesus because He fills us with life to keep our mind and body strong. God is essential, like food, for keeping us alive and well. Food will not last, but God is forever.

Breaking News – Very important news that the TV or radio immediately announces to the world to keep people updated on what is happening on Earth.

Business – A group that buys and/or sells a certain thing, or a number of things in order to make money. Businesses provide goods and services that make everyone's life easier. They can also help people in need and make the world run a little smoother.

Business Owner – An owner of a particular business; people who provide goods and services. In order for the economy to be healthy, business owners are needed.

Callings – The plans and desires that God has planted in your heart that will lead you and encourage you to make the world a better place to live in.

Cheerful Giver – One who has a positive attitude and loves to do things to help others. One who recognizes that all of the good things we have in life are from God and that it pleases Him when we share with others.

Chef – People who prepare food into a variety of dishes. Those who are knowledgeable about food groups, nutrition, and many recipes in order to create healthy meals for people. Chefs can release life through the food they provide.

Children with Purpose – You are a child with purpose! God gave you dreams and goals and He wants you to use everything you have to help many people. God wants you to spread the Good News about His Son, Jesus, and to love one another with a very big heart.

Church – A place where people come together and sing songs to God, learn about God, and spend time together honoring God.

Circumstance – An event or situation that you might find yourself in. It can be good or bad, but in every circumstance we have to remember to trust God and ask Him to guide us.

City – A large town that many people live and work in. Every state has lots of different cities.

Co-labor – To work together with someone.

Commandments – Rules that were made with love. When we follow God's commandments, He is very happy and our lives will be blessed.

Communication – To talk to someone in person, on the phone, or through the mail; to share a message over the TV, in a movie, or over the radio.

Computer – An electronic device that connects people from around the world. It holds a great amount of information and can do a lot of amazing tasks. Computers allow people to communicate with each other, create things, and solve problems that the human brain might not be able to do on its own.

Construction Worker –People who build homes and business buildings. Every house and building that you see in your neighborhood was built by construction workers. They show people what it means to work hard and get positive results.

Continent – A big body of land where a lot of different people live. There are seven continents on this earth: Africa, Antarctica, Asia, Australia, Europe, North America, and South America.

Counselors – People who gather wisdom from the heart of God and help guide a person to the correct path for their life. Counselors help people through tough times and in happy times. They are similar to teachers and pastors.

Country – Cities and states make up a country. A lot of people live in a country; they follow rules and laws set by their nation's leaders. The main leader of a country can be called a president or a king.

Courageous – Fearlessness; we can be courageous because we know that God is with us all the time. It means doing the right thing even when it seems too hard.

Creation – The universe and everything inside of it – including the world, people, animals, stars, and planets. God created everything.

Creativity – To design and make new and original pieces of art. Creativity is a gift from God and adds joy and life to the world.

Culture – The beliefs and customs of a nation or people. Culture creates a standard of thought and feelings for people to live by, i.e. "This is a culture of love and honor."

Dancer – A form of art in which a person moves the body in a rhythmic way, often to music. Dancers are flexible and creative in their dance styles. They express beauty and emotion through their motions and gestures. God loves it when people use their body to glorify Him.

Desire – An emotion that expresses wanting something; it can express the feeling of caring and compassion that God put within us. God also has desires. For example, God desires us to love Him and others.

Destiny – A course of events or happenings that follows God's plan. The things that will happen in your future are your destiny, according to God's plan.

Director – Those who direct, or lead in the production of movies, music, TV shows, writing projects, and more. They take creative thoughts and make it into a complete piece of art. They have an understanding of leadership and teamwork.

Discernment – To have a good sense of the things going on around you and to be aware of your surroundings. Discernment helps you make good decisions. It is important to have this quality so that you act with love and honor, which furthers the Kingdom of God.

Earthly Father – The father that the Lord gave you who watches over you, instructs you, and protects you on

Earth. God made earthly fathers to be a good example of what God is like.

Elijah – A prophet of God in the Old Testament who served God faithfully and performed miracles. He was sometimes afraid, but he trusted God. He did amazing things with God's help and God did amazing things for Elijah.

Elisha – A prophet who obeyed everything that God said and performed many miracles on Earth. He was a leader and a good example of what it means to be a servant of God.

Emotions – The feelings you get inside, such as happiness, sadness, anger, excitement, or loneliness. People such as School Counselors help others understand and deal with their emotions. Emotions are usually a response to an event in your life, and it is important to talk with God about your emotions because He loves to know how you feel. Jesus is the best Counselor.

Encourager – Someone who lifts another person up with their words. Encouragers are kind and compassionate and they support their friends in every way they can. They have a positive attitude and are ready to help whenever they are needed.

Enemies – People that try to harm you. God tells us to forgive our enemies and show them love even when it is hard.

Evangelists – Those who bring people together and tell them about Jesus. They tell people about Jesus' gift of salvation and show the world the true nature of God. They care for the poor and needy, and are leaders of inviting people into God's eternal Kingdom.

Faithful – To be reliable and trustworthy; to obey what God tells you to do.

Firefighter – Those who fight fires and rescue people from storms and fires. They are very important in the Mountain of Government because they save people that we love and things that we care for. Firefighters are courageous.

Freedom – The ability to do whatever you want. True freedom is following God's plan and living under His protective and watchful care. God has given us freedom to make our own choices and He wants each and every person to use that freedom to spread love throughout the world.

Fruit of Good Work – When you do good actions and help those in need, amazing things will happen in your life. God rewards those serve Him with "good fruit." All who listen to Him and take care of His children will be blessed greatly by God.

Generations – The amount of time between the birth of a parent and the birth of their children, usually between 18 and 25 years.

Gifts – God has given every single person on the earth one or more special gifts. It is up to you to pray to God and ask Him what special gift He has given you and then use that gift to make the world a better place. God has also given us many other gifts, like life on Earth, our family, and Jesus.

Glory – To give great praise and honor to someone. For example, King David had a director of music that helped him to sing the glory of God and creation. Glory is a positive thing as it can show forth the beauty of all that God has done.

Grace – To forgive and to show love even when someone does something you may not like. They may not deserve it, but God teaches us that grace helps us love others better.

Gracious – To be forgiving and caring; to do what is right. When someone wrongs us, we must be gracious and forgive, just as Jesus forgave us.

Hair Stylist – Someone who cuts or styles hair in order to help improve their image. These people are creative, and often understanding and good listeners. They are faithful to their customers and love to work with others.

Healing – To make whole and clean again; to cure someone of sickness, sadness, or bad feelings. There can be healing of the mind, body, and spirit. All healing comes from God because He wants His children to be healthy.

Heartfelt – Deeply felt; something coming from strong emotion. A person who has a positive and caring attitude that wants to help other people in need.

Heaven – God lives in our hearts and in the world around us, but Heaven is a place where God also lives. There is no more sadness or bad things in Heaven. Heaven is a perfect place.

Heavenly – To be of God, having godly characteristics and qualities. To care about the things God cares about and act in a way that is pleasing to Him.

Heavenly Father – God is our Father in Heaven who watches over, guides, and protects us. We may not see Him like we see an earthly father, but our Heavenly Father is always present. He cares about what we care about and loves it when we talk with Him.
Heavenly Perspective – A focus that is set on thinking about God's will and how He wants things to be done here on Earth.
Hollywood – A big city in the state of California where movies and music are made. A lot of people want to work there to act in or make movies because the people who work there are often well known and make a lot of money.
Holy Spirit – The spirit of God here on Earth that lives inside of you and all around you. The Holy Spirit instructs you on how to make good decisions and leads you on the correct path of life.
Honor – To have respect for someone. It is important to treat friends, parents, babysitters, and pastors with honor and respect. When you honor those around you, you honor God, too.
Hopeful – To be happy for the future and not afraid about any part of life because God has it all under control. God wants us to have hope and think positively about the things to come.
Humanity – Every person on earth that God created.
Humility – To not take credit for yourself, but to remember that all good things come from Jesus.
Imagination – The creativity and wonder that God put inside of our heads and hearts to create amazing images and fun things. Imagination makes the world a fun place to live in. It brings life and color to the world.
Individual Expression – An individual's unique creations and ideas. God gave you individual expression to show the world the wonderful things that only you can do. Individual expression is a beautiful thing that we should all be thankful for and use to glorify God.
Instruments – Tools that people play on to create beautiful sounds and music. Some examples of instruments are a piano, guitar, flute, and violin.
Jesus – God's only Son, sent from Heaven. He lived a perfect life here on Earth and is the best example on how to live our own lives. He loves us so much that He gave up His own life so that every person who loves Him can live with God forever in Heaven.
Justice – Something that is done with fairness and equality. God sees and knows everything and He will make sure everything on Earth is done with justice.
Kindhearted – To have a gentle, caring spirit that loves other people and cares for those around you. To have a positive attitude and be willing to give of time and goods in order to help others.
King David – A king from the Old Testament who loved God and wrote many songs. King David celebrated the beauty of heaven and loved to praise God through song and dance.
Kings – Rulers over a group of people that care for a country and make future plans for the country. Kings protect and serve people and have a lot of responsibility.
Lawmakers – Those who make laws. Lawmakers can create laws with righteousness and justice. They protect and serve everyone who is under their government.
Laws – There are heavenly laws and earthly laws. Laws in our country are rules that are put together from the government to help everyone have a safe and happy life.
Leaders – Those who are gifted in leading others in small or big ways. These people can encourage others to live for God. They can help many people when they show them the right way to live and are good examples of how God would have them act on this Earth.
Librarian – Those who work in libraries and care for books and historical records. They gather the story of humanity and make it available for all to see. They are collectors of wisdom and keepers of God's Word. Librarians love to capture fantasy, creativity, and the wonderful works found in the Bible.
Life Lessons and Trials – Things that happen in life that seem very hard and may make you sad. Life Lessons challenge you and also teach you something when you overcome them. No life lesson or trial is too hard when you have God on your side!
Love – A strong, positive feeling for another person or thing. God first showed us love by sending his Son, Jesus, to the world. Love is the positive way we feel towards our family and friends. Love creates good things.
Majestic – Something that is beautiful, grand, amazing. Every day God releases majestic art in the sky, which

displays His power and beauty.

Mary – The mother of Jesus. She believed in Jesus' greatness before anyone else did. She saw hope and love in her Son's future and prepared Him for greatness.

Medicine – Something that is used to make a person healthy again. Medicine helps heal people from diseases, injuries, pain, and other things that hurt the body. God put medicine on this Earth to help His children if they are feeling sick or if their body is hurting.

Melodies – The musical sounds that come out of an instrument or someone's singing voice. Melodies are beautiful and bring joy to people who listen to them.

Messengers – People who are sent out to deliver news. God's children are called to be messengers of the good news of His love and salvation.

Miracles – Amazing, good, wonderful acts or events that happen from the power of God.

Mission Trip – A trip that people go on to share what the Bible says to people who do not know God yet. Mission trips are very important for spreading the Good News of Jesus Christ and to let the world know the good things that God has done for us. Mission trips do not have to be far; you can go on a mission trip in your own city!

Money – Coins or paper bills used to buy things like food, clothes, or books.

Mother – The woman that God chose to take care of you and love you. They are the glue that holds the family together. They understand their children's needs and desires. They are a picture of the love that we receive from Heaven.

Mountain of Celebration – The place where people come to have fun with life. It is the home of creativity, laughter, life, and joyful noises. God gave us celebration so that we may praise Him for the beautiful works of art that He put on this earth.

Mountain of Economy – The place where people build businesses and make or use money. Every country has an economy, and every country needs help growing their economy. This is also an important place for learning to give money to those in need.

Mountain of Education – The place where people learn. Any time someone is receiving knowledge, especially in school, they are getting an education. Education teaches people skills that help them have a better life. It teaches people to make the world a better place to live.

Mountain of Family – The relatives that God has placed in your life, such as mothers, fathers, brothers, sisters, aunts, uncles and grandparents. God gave us family to protect us, love us, and help us not to be lonely.

Mountain of Government – The place where our laws come from. This place provides safety and protection from bad people. The government also helps give us a peaceful city because of its workers and helpful laws.

Mountain of Media – This is the place where people hear about what is happening in the world. The Mountain of Media leads in giving people news. It involves communication through technology and provides you with your favorite TV shows and movies.

Mountain of Religion – This is the place where people learn of and hold a specific belief system. There are many religions, but only one religion takes you to Jesus. If you follow Jesus, you are a Christian. Christians are meant to love Jesus and obey what He says.

Music – Sounds with different tones and rhythms that people listen to for enjoyment. King David was a person who made beautiful music and played it before God to celebrate His amazing wonders!

Nanny – Nannies help care for and raise children that are not their own. They have the gift of helping others and servant-hood. Nannies assist parents in being successful by taking care of their children. Nannies are very helpful to families that have working parents.

Nation – A community of people who live in a certain area and usually have a common background, language, culture, and government.

Navy – The naval (ocean-going) warfare service branch of a nation. These people, like firefighters, would give their life to save another. They are strong and protect their families and countries from harm.

News Anchors – People who present news during news broadcasting. They are the face of the Mountain of Media. They are gifted communicators. They tell people important news and inform us about life. They care for the world a lot and want everyone to be safe and uplifted by the stories they share.

Nurse – A person trained to care for the sick or disabled. They have gifts of compassion and patience. They bring health and wholeness to people in pain and in need. Nurses are hard workers that put others before themselves. They partner with Jesus on a daily basis to restore people to health through healing, miracles and medicine.

Nurture – To be extra kind and caring towards someone. To nurture means to protect and watch over someone you love or someone in need out of the goodness of your heart. Parents are a good example of people who nurture.

Painter – Someone who paints, usually referring to an artist who creates pictures with paint. They are creative visionaries that paint beauty onto a canvas. They are extremely talented and look to Heaven for inspiration.

Parenting – The act of raising children. Parenting is what your mom and dad do to keep you safe and on the right path to happiness. Parenting involves a lot of love, nurturing, and protecting. God gifted the parents of the world this trait so they may know how to take care of their children.

Pastoral Heart – To have a heart that loves others no matter what the situation is. A pastoral heart is nurturing, loving, and protecting. People with pastoral hearts care for the broken, hungry, wounded, and needy.

Pastors – Those who preach in a church and tell others about God and truths from the Bible. They care for those in their church and for others as a mother bird cares for her chicks. Their hearts go out to the lost and they desire to bring spiritual health to every family. The earth is a blessed place because of pastors and what they do.

Patience – A willingness to wait in a spirit of grace and trust. It can involve helping others even when it is inconvenient for you. It involves having a gentle and loving heart. It sometimes means to endure trouble or hardship without getting angry or upset.

Peace – Being free from any sad or troubling thoughts or events in your life. Peace brings out happiness and freedom. Peace means to be calm and relaxed, knowing that you are safe, even if everything in your life is not perfect.

Perfect Will of God – This is what God desires to have happen here on Earth. He wants what is good and happy to happen to all humans. His plan for each and every person is perfect, and we must listen to what God has to say for our lives so that His will can be accomplished.

Perspective – A certain way of thinking about something. When we have a heavenly perspective, we are thinking about how God wants us to act and how we can best spread God's Word throughout the world.

Pianist – A pianist is someone who plays the piano. They are so skillful with this instrument that they can make wonderful music by moving their fingers. People who play the piano and other instruments give the world creative songs from Heaven.

Piano – An instrument with a number of keys that play different sounds when you press them. A pianist plays the piano and creates beautiful tunes for people to listen, sing, and dance to.

Praying/To Pray – Praying is when you talk with God. God knows what you want in your heart, but He loves it when you talk to Him in prayer. Praying can mean saying thank you to God, asking Him for help, or just telling Him about your day.

President – Those who lead a nation. Their job is to make sure people take care of the Earth and give it to Jesus as a gift. They care about everyone and want to protect the people who live in their country. They have a lot of responsibility, but their strength and courage helps them be servants of God.

Principal – The leader of a school. They are like our parents when we are at school. Principals are gifted and entrusted to care for many children. They guide young people through life lessons and trials, and keep a school running properly.

Professor – Another name for a professor is a teacher. They spend their time teaching and educating others. Professors are always available to help, always have a positive attitude, and want all their students to succeed. Every godly professor and teacher gets their good ideas from Jesus, the master Teacher.

Prophetic Voices – Words that speak truth and life and joy into people's lives by hearing from God and sharing His will and voice with others. A prophet is an example of someone who speaks prophetic voices into the lives of people.

Prophets – Those who help us to hear the heart of God. They are a gift to the body of Christ. Prophets speak words of peace and bring Heaven's heart to the earth. They are amazing people because they desire to hear and speak what God has to say to us. They can see what is possible for the future and work to make it possible today.

Prosper – To succeed in something and be successful; to further the Kingdom of God. It is a very good thing and helps people to be happy.

Protection – The act of being kept safe and free from harm. God's strong arms offer the best protection.

Radio Host – Those who share their voice on talk shows and radio shows. They present music and often have a good sense of humor and speak on topics of interest. They are encouragers at heart and love to spread good news. They want the world to be inspired by the music and words that they share.

Radio Shows – A radio show is similar to a talk show except that you can only listen to the people talking; you cannot see them. A Radio Host leads a Radio Show and they make people happy when they share good news.

Reliable – Someone who can be trusted and is available to help anyone in need.

Reporter – Those who speak about what happens to people all over the world. They want to see the truth in every person and situation. Reporters are servants at heart and desire to see the bad things of the world come to an end.

Resources – A certain amount of materials, information, money, or other goods that people can go to when they need something.

Restoration – To make something beautiful, whole, and the way it was originally intended to be. People like apostles have a heart for restoration because they want God to be glorified all through the earth, which is the way it is supposed to be.

Righteousness – The character trait of doing what is right and truthful in the eyes of God. Righteousness brings honor to God and to those around you when you display this trait with a loving heart.

Routine – The things and habits people do in their everyday lives.

Sacrifice – To give something up even when you may not want to. It means offering something to God or someone else because of the love you have in your heart. Jesus was the Ultimate Sacrifice and He gave up His life so that all who believe in Him may live with God forever.

Salvation – To believe that Jesus is God's Son and that He came to Earth to save us from our sins. Salvation is the path to Heaven. Jesus promises we will be with Him forever through salvation.

School Counselor – Those who help people understand and deal with their emotions, feelings, and path in life. Counselors help people make good decisions, especially when they gather wisdom from the heart of God. They teach, nurture, and love those who come to them.

Sculptor – A sculptor is an artist who creates shapes and molds of beautiful designs and people. They are creative and talented in what they do. They love to work for the glory of God and show people the beautiful things that the Lord has put on this Earth.

Security – To feel protected and taken care of.

Selfless – To put someone else's needs before your own.

Servant-hood – To listen and obey everything that God tells you to do, even when you do not understand why. Servant-hood is an important trait to have because it not only helps other people, but it also sets you on the right path towards God.

Servants – Those who help and serve others with love and care in their hearts. They do not worry about whether or not they will receive a prize in return, but they work for the good of others.

Seven Mountains – God placed the Seven Mountains in the heart of man. These mountains include a model for Education, Government, Religion, Media, Economy, Family, and Celebration. The Lord wants us to bring change and discipleship to the world. He gives us solutions to the world's problems for every aspect of life. The gifts and abilities that God has blessed us with should be used to influence and change the Seven Mountains to bring God's glory to Earth.

Shepherd – One who cares for sheep. Shepherds are caring and they protect their flock. God is the Ultimate Shepherd. He guides us through life and keeps us safe. Shepherds watch over their sheep and make sure they do not stray. In the same way, God watches over you and makes sure you follow the path of life.

Singer – One who sings. Singers can bring forth the symphony of Heaven through all different types of music. They can sing to the Lord a new song and the earth celebrates. Singers release heavenly emotion and love through their songs. Soccer Player –Athletic people who play soccer. Soccer Players fit in the Mountain of Celebration because they bring a lot of fun and excitement to people. They are strong, agile, and quick.

Social Worker – Those who care for others, especially small and vulnerable children. They desire justice, freedom, and a wonderful life for every human. They give their lives to place children in loving homes that care for their every need.

Songwriter – One who writes songs and often puts them to music. They give people an opportunity to celebrate. They write words to songs so that people can sing along and dance to music. God loves it when we make songs that worship Him.

Spiritual Health – The act of living a healthy and complete life, filled with the presence of God. When your spiritual health is in balance, you feel joy and love and peace. In the same way that you take care of your body by eating healthy, spiritual health is cared for by praying, reading the Bible, and spending time with people who love you and Jesus.

State – A certain area where a lot of people live and follow laws set by the president and local lawmakers.

Supportive – To help another person and to provide positive encouragement in the lives of those around you.

Survival – The act of living, breathing, and remaining in a state of wellness. Food and water is important for survival because they keep our bodies running.

Talk Show – A television show in which people discuss different topics and share with the world lots of different events and information. They have the ability to share good news and make people happy.

Teachers – Those who teach others. They help people to obtain knowledge in many areas of life; they can teach about God and show people the correct way to live. They also teach others how to love and how to hear God.

Teamwork – To work together with other people to accomplish a job or play a game. Teamwork is an important thing because it teaches you how to get along with others and it makes everyone happy.

Technology – Tools that help people communicate easier. Some examples of technology are computers, radios, televisions, and phones. Technology makes tasks easier. It is helpful for spreading the Good News of God because it helps us to reach out to many people very fast.

Testimony – Someone's personal story. The greatest testimony is the beautiful story of God and how He sent His Son to Earth to love and rescue people. A testimony tells other people about your faith and praises God through words and actions.

The Kingdom – The place where God reigns as King over Heaven and Earth. It is like God's very big house and He wants to share it with you!

The Ultimate Pastor – Earthly Pastors model after the Ultimate Pastor, Jesus, in that they are caring and protective. They nurture and love people no matter what the situation may be. Earthly Pastors look to Jesus as the best example on how to live their lives.

To be Saved – To believe that Jesus Christ is God's one true Son and that He came to Earth to save all humans. When we have Jesus in our hearts, God promises we will live a happy life with Him forever.

To Rescue – To save someone from harms way; to let someone know how much God loves them and wants them to follow what He says.

To Serve – To put time and energy into helping others in need. It means to put someone else's needs or wants before your own. This pleases God greatly.

To Worship/Worshiper – To say "thank you" to God by singing, dancing, praying, or even writing. A worshiper loves God with all of his or her heart and wants to celebrate all of the wonderful things that He has done!

Truth – That which is right and holy and true in God's eyes. Truth sets people free and gives people joy and contentment.

Unity – To work together peacefully with someone or something. When a group of people get along with each other and agree with things, they have unity. It is important that team members have unity to peacefully complete a job.

Victory –To win a battle or a struggle. It helps people go far in life; it is important to give thanks to God for every victory in your life.

Vision – An image that you get in your mind about something that you want to happen that glorifies God. A godly vision sets people on the right path towards God and leads people to have success in their life.

Visionaries – People who see the good in the future and turn the beauty of Heaven into reality. They have a positive outlook on life and work to build a healthy environment for everyone around them.

Visionary – Someone who sees things the way Jesus sees things. Visionaries have a big heart and want things to go the way that God has planned.

Vulnerable – People that can easily be harmed, such as those who might be too weak to protect themselves. For example, vulnerable children need to be cared for by parents, Social Workers, or nannies.

Wealth – To have a large amount of money or other resources. Wealth is usually related to having a lot of money, but you can also be wealthy with the treasures God has stored up for you in Heaven! That is the greatest kind of wealth.

Wholeness – To be healthy and complete, free of sickness or other bad things.

Wisdom – That which helps people to make good decisions and to serve and teach others with that knowledge. All wisdom comes from God. Some examples of people who have wisdom are teachers, parents, pastors, librarians, and counselors.

World Changer – Someone who knows who they are in Jesus and partners with God to make lasting change on the earth, in their job, and in the lives of people.

Writer – Those who tell the story of life through words. They like to journal about the things that God has done. They desire to let everyone know about their creative imagination. They can change the world through passionate writing.

ChildrenWithPurpose.com

For more Illustrations by E. M. M. Clonts, please visit:

www.facebook.com/pages/EMM-Illustrate/178142495537491
emm.illustrate@gmail.com

Made in the USA
San Bernardino, CA
29 May 2016